Are you the REAL Santa Claus?

Are you the REAL Santa Claus?

This book is for all the children of the world…

no matter what age you think you are.

Am I the real Santa Claus?

Well, I am here to see and be with you,

to take a photo, and to tell me what you would like for Christmas.

My question for you is,

who do you think Santa is?

Santa knows about children and what they really want… Love.

Do you know why?

Because Santa represents Love and Magic for all Children…

regardless of their age.

Santa shows hope and goodness

and to remind you to always be kind to everyone and everything.

He does that by using <u>Christmas Magic</u> to teach you the art of

goodness and giving.

Santa loves to give gifts whether it is just a kind word,

a blessing of hope, or something sweet and fun!

Now I know that you see lots of people dressed in Red and fur,

a stocking cap!... and of course, boots!

At the North Pole, where my home is,

I dress warmly and always wear my boots when it is snowy or cold, or really, any type of weather!

It is through Christmas Magic that you see so many Santas,

because there are many little boys and girls who love Santa.

There is a special Santa for every special child!

So regardless of how many there are,

there is always a special Santa just for you!

To know which Santa is the REAL Santa,

you will know in your heart the one that is your special Santa Claus.

If you believe in Santa, I go by many different names and appearances like:

Father Christmas

Papa Noel

St. Nicholas

Christkind

Chris Cringle

Babouschka

Sinter Klass

and the one and only, Santa Claus

So, if you ask, "Am I the real Santa Claus?"

Why of course I am,

Because you believe in me,

and I believe in YOU.

J. P. "Pete" Mitchell – Pete started his career working in video production and Halloween events in 1972. Pete channeled his passion for helping others into a career. In '74 he became an Emergency Medical Technician in the State of Georgia. Unhappy with the way training was done, he developed a makeup application he called "Special Trauma" to teach first responders what a trauma scene looked like. Soon he was immersed in the world of production and hands on training. The makeup application developed from a hobby to a second career and so realistic Pete won an NATAS Emmy. Pete also provided his creative skills in Halloween production and developing events in theme parks. His involvement in video production evolved into Motion pictures. His Son Jeremiah studied editing and producing and joined the company to create JPM Television. Pete was asked to have his friend Santa Claus with him for visits with children who did not really know "the real Santa". From community programs, private events, and "The Limelight" in Atlanta, to the Macy's Thanksgiving Day Parade in New York, Pete and Santa have toured throughout the country to visit adults and children in schools, theaters and hospitals. The one question always asked is, "Are you the REAL Santa Claus", and the response is in this book. Enjoy and Peace.

Liza Petruzzo - Liza Petruzzo is a comic artist and illustrator from the wilds of New England who loves to capture the magic of this world and the next. She has sharpened her pens under the tutelage of the Center of Cartoon Studies and probably thinks you're very nice. Santa found Liza on one of his visits in New England and asked her personally to create the illustrations for his book. "I think she captured Santa in a very kind and realistic light".

www.ingramcontent.com/pod-product-compliance
Lightning Source LLC
Chambersburg PA
CBHW051351110526
44591CB00025B/2972